© 2022 All rights reserved. No part of this publication may be reproduced, scanned distributed, or transmitted in any form or by any means, including photocopying, recording, or other electronic or mechanical methods, without the prior written permission of the publisher, except in the case of brief quotations embodied in critical reviews and certain other noncommercial uses permitted by copyright law. Thank you for buying an authorized edition of this book and for complying with copyright laws.

Manufactured in the United States

Any resemblance to actual events or persons, living or dead, is entirely coincidental. This is in no form meant for harm nor do we promote harm. Personal perspective use only. Please do not copy/mimic any words or illustration from this book.

Illustrations by Cameron Wilson for Soulsimplicity Design and Publishing.

LOYAL T AND DESTINY LETTERS TO THE WORLD

BY TY LOYD-CALHOUN AND DESTINY

ILLUSTRATED BY CAMERON WILSON

My Dream Is

Now when you look at me
you would see that I have
pointy elf ears
or a mole on my nose
or even short and stubby fingernails
but one thing that I have that you probably can't see
is a dream
A dream that isn't just for me but it's for all
A dream that addresses issues that are big that some people see as small
A dream that doesn't matter what you look like short or tall
Now if you are close to me you might see that I am
kind
brave
and respectful
but one thing that you probably can't see
is a dream
A dream that stands high but still gets ignored
A dream that leaves some people bored
A dream that I will continue to ask for
This dream is equality between us
the restoration of our now dirty Earth
and the stopping of violence
not all dreams come true but I have a chance
to give these dreams
at least one glance.

-By Destiny

Visionary sight

My dreams are bigger than the eye can see
It's a gift and a curse, I'm blessed to see what no one else can see
But I'm cursed to see them alone I find
I want to extend my visions further than my mind
Sometimes I seek acceptance from others who can not see
They can not see themselves make it so they don't believe
This is like expecting someone to see clear thru your glasses
It's impossible unless they're sight and yours matches
When they try to see your visions it will strain their vision
And cause unnecessary blurry discomfort, the opposite of precision.
Their vision is blurred because they were never met to wear your glasses
Sometimes you vision is as tall as a giraffes is
They can not give you any instruction
On your life's prescription
Their negative advice is nothing to go by
That's like a turtle listening when you tell it to fly
Sometimes there will be obstacles in your way
Get over them and don't worry about what they say
I call this cleaning your dirty glasses
Wipe away, wipe away so your vision can shine to the masses
Not always is sharing caring
SEEKING LOVE IN THE WRONG PLACES CAN BE OVERBEARING
Sometimes you have to wear your glasses proud
And cheer for you when no one is around
Everyone should plan for the future with their wisdom and imagination
It can either fail miserably or work brilliantly
But you have one life so why not try to see your visions through
In order to see your visions become reality you'll have to do what you have to do.

-By Loyal T

Inner Child

We are all YOUNGSTARS of the wild
Inside all of us is a **Inner child**
You see as a child you may not know
As a kid the things you do and hear affects how you GROW

We are all YOUNGSTARS in space
To become a planet, sun or moon is life's race
Nothing can grow in the same place
I dare you to open your mind about the human race

You see I have seen adults suffer in life
Because a piece of their childhood wasn't right
Not all pain leaves visible scars
Dealing with life can be a real fight not a spar

There is a saying "sticks and stones hurt but words will never"
This person must have not been verbally abused ever.
Like trees It takes seconds to cut one down
And a lifetime to grow from the ground.

Life is about growth, no one ever stops growing up
So your Inner child is always there even when you're an adult
So think about as a child what brought you Joy and pain
Remember everything that brought you sunshine in the rain

These things that gave you sunshine
Will give you strength and peace so never leave it behind
Anything that gave you pain you should reconcile
To feel serenity, just tap into your **Inner child**.

-By Loyal T

October is Bully Prevention Month

Teachers say be nice
and play fair
but sadly I never see this anywhere
I see cruelty and rude stares

You may be thinking what is she saying?
or "Oh we were just playing!"
but that's not what the victim is conveying

October is bullying prevention month
instead of being mean
tell someone that they're enough
and that they reign King or Queen

You know that it's right
so don't cause a fight
stop causing fright
and think about this tonight

If someone wants to bully you
how would you feel
if someone were to bully you
would fear be something you feel.

-By Destiny

YinYin

I'm a solid water cube but ice I would never call myself
If you wanna call me something call me YinYin if it helps
YinYin
is ice nigerian

I"m pure and needed in life
I'll melt in your hand in daylight
But lately that's not the case
See right now I'm YinYin in muddy water in earth's vase

My touch could soothe a pain
Muddy water is my environment I'm engulfed in

It's hard to be solid in a toxic place
But I can adapt anywhere even space
With mud around me it's hard to see
Truly how pure I am-really

I don't let my environment
Change who I am

The inside of me may be cloudy
Because inside of me I am bubbly
I keep it cloudy so you do not confuse
I keep it cloudy so I do not get misused
I never been soft always hard
When I hail from the sky I'll dent your car

Taking me out of the vase may be hard you see
Because the mudd makes me slippery
Do not hold me too tight

I can cause a little frostbite
Taken out of earth's vase you see
Rinse with holy water the mud slides off of me
Now that I'm out I'm dangerous again
An intelligent black man is black YinYin

-By Loyal T

Big Brown

Your big brown eyes
Like the soil of the earth
Your beautiful black skin
Really shows your worth

Your curly kinky hair
Flies in the wind
As you keep your head up
And raise your chin

Others might hate
Or throw shade
But keep shining a smile
Show them that their too late

They're too late to bring you down
Because you are already to far up
You watch as the haters frown
Because you know that you're enough

-By Destiny

I'm Me

I'm not an oreo, I'm me
You don't have to smell my teen spirit to see

Just because I'm black
Why do you judge that I can't listen to other things than rap
Music is my thing, but I'm not a singer
My question is, Do you have to make it linger?

I'm not an oreo, I'm me
What I got is a blvd of broken dreams you see

For a long time I was crawling in the dark
Looking for an Oasis Wonderwall in Abe Linkin Park
I find it ironic, when I don't speak
I have no doubt I can't compete

I'm not an oreo, I'm me
You oughta know I'm not a loser baby
I'm not Jeremy but I'm well spoken
lady
When I come around your purse doesn't need to be choking
Just because I am an American reject
Doesn't mean I am not a foo fighter Hanging by a moment

I'm not an Oreo I'm me
I've never been an American idiot
you see

I can't be the only one tired of people getting the best of you
By the way this the reason I do what I do
Rhyming alt artist and songs is how you remind me
All the small things as a kid that made me

I'm not an Oreo, I'm me
This poem has put my soul in a heart shaped box you see

When I walk in the store outside the city with one hand in my pocket
Just know I'm one of two princes and not a threat
Popo when you see me driving with one headlight
I'm hoping it's not closing time and you don't end my semi-charmed life

I'm not an Oreo, I'm me
I often feel like a cage elephant, that the riptide broke free

The song sound of change, I love the penmanship
Reminds me of somebody that I used to know that was radioactive
And that's me and day one's we always been royals
Bringing the thunder and never disloyal.

I'm not an Oreo, I'm me
I may be the black modern day Buddy Holly

I'm just walkin on the sun showing my scar tissue
But even though I am my own worst enemy I remember that nothing compares to you
The one who listened to my bittersweet Symphony
And know thru it all you know now I'm not an Oreo, I'm me.

-By Loyal T

Black Skin

Black skin is not a badge of shame
Black skin is glorious
Black skin is what makes fame
it's what makes me notorious

Although it may be judged
it's beautiful to me
and it won't be changed above
it's the thing that makes me feel free

And if you have a problem then oh well
I will never break a sweat
That is because my skin always rings a bell
you're just mad that you've never seen anything like this yet

But I will start to be humble
because I know you're probably done
just know that black will never tumble
also I think being black is rather fun

Love your melanin
It's a part of you
nothing will be better than
you knowing that you rule

-By Destiny

Interior vs Exterior

Exterior vs Interior you can't naturally change either
But which one do you think makes you better
Some people change the exterior
Just like seasons or the weather
Your lips or nose size are exterior
Things you're born with like your hair texture
Just like your skin you don't choose so how does it make you better
understand this poem is not a lecture
It is my way of showing you what's for sure
No one chooses their skin
But some people dwell on outside to have pride within.
it's the inside that makes us
We are all human beings and nothing above
We all have bones, we all have blood
We all are the same inside and want to be loved
We all have a heart and lungs
But instead of looking at what makes us the same we rather judge
We all have a brain and feet
My mind stands for love and I can't be discrete
There are many natural things that make us the same
Before the 1600's race wasn't a thing
We were all human beings
Let's make unity a daily routine
Just like we all have belly buttons
Daily help someone different going thru something
Divided we fall, together we conquer
So why are we at odds with each other
So I ask you What's more important exterior or interior beauty
What makes us the same, more of our exterior or interior beauty
To me it's clear our interior is what keeps us the same
But I wonder which one you choose in your Brain?

-By Loyal T

My Parents

My parents can be strict
but they also can be nice
and they add a little kick
to a boring normal life

they tell me that I'm smart
and that I'm beautiful
they've been helpful from the start
and for that I'll always be grateful

they tried to give me things
that they didn't have as a child
they will almost always try to pull the strings
to ensure that I have a smile

they tell me that I'm inspiring
and that I have a lot of talent
my joys never expiring
and I'm always ready for a challenge

I love my parents
for things they say and do
because I know that they swear
that what they say is true

-By Destiny

The Only Hood I Claim

The only hood I claim is fatherhood
In this hood I rep to be great and not good
I stand tall there as I should
My love is the only weapon that gets pulled

The streets is nothing I would ever claim
I ride for my kids because they have my last name
I brought them to life I have to guide them in life's game
I want to teach them to manifest to become acclaim

I teach my kids not to rob, steal, or kill for Dinero
When it's all said and done
I'm my daughters' first love and my son's first hero
I'm trying to teach them to give 100 percent and not zero

They are a branch from my stem
They are my offspring, but I have to spring to things important to them.
I grow as they grow so things I can't do what I did back then
For them I stopped those things I will never do it again

Fatherhood to me is teaching by example
If I don't tell the truth, when they lie I can't get mad at the rascal
You word is your born on my block is substantial
This is why on Christmas for the toys I scramble

I am the male Parent
Keeping promises is important to an adolescent
On my block me, them, and their mother are interdependent
The only hood I claim is fatherhood and I hope that's apparent
So if you have kids forget about your street credit

Do what it takes to get good credit
Show them how to love so they won't be a misfit
When you claim fatherhood you want your family to be well-knit.

-By Loyal T

The Interstate of Life

Learning to drive is one thing
Knowing the Interstate of life will widen your growth ring

No one is the best driver on their first drive
This takes experience and time

On the interstate of life you will need confidence to get off your block
Without that you should keep the car in park

Confidence is a basic key you need I will admit to be alright
Learning to drive is having the confidence to take control, to move forward in life

Controlling your emotions, body feelings, or thoughts to stay safe
See that's knowing what's your interstate

Once you are fully confident in the neighborhood and getting around
Then you can try the interstate to get out of town

A few things you should know before leaving your driveway
Peace is not merely avoidance of the negativity

It's knowing that the interstate of life has highs and lows
But progesive way is to take the highway and not the low way

When getting to that on ramp
Stay calm this is no time to panic

You'll have to pick up your speed
Going too slow will get you hurt indeed

When leaving the on ramp look cars when entering the interstate
This will determine the speed you need to create

Once on the interstate don't go slow or speed too fast it's not a race
Go with the flow of traffic but at your own pace

It's important to travel in your own lane
Going to too fast, you can loose control and be left with deathly pain

Also going too fast can get you pulled over and ticketed by a governing force
So controlling your inter-state on the interstate is the source

You see on the interstate of life there will be people that will move negatively faster
And some that move slower, but doing what you are comfortable with is better

You can't go too slow or you'll be left behind
Left behind by changing times

In life there are many times to achieve greatness
you will have to leave your comfort zone
But while you are driving stay focus on your goal to make it safely home

Everyone learns their inter-state better
The more and more they come back
Eventually as you drive you will know when you are the leader of the pack

When you lead the pack you fully know your inter-state
Living to be the best is one's greatest fate

-By Loyal T